THERE ARE 344 KINDS
OF DOGS IN THE WORLD.

BUT WHEN YOU REALLY GET DOWN TO IT,
THERE ARE ONLY TWO KINDS
OF DOGS THAT MATTER...

Shiba-Inus are majestic and strong.

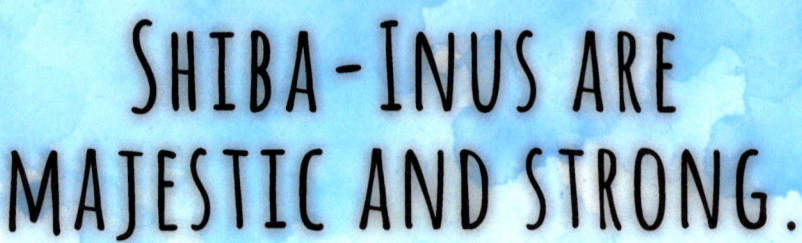

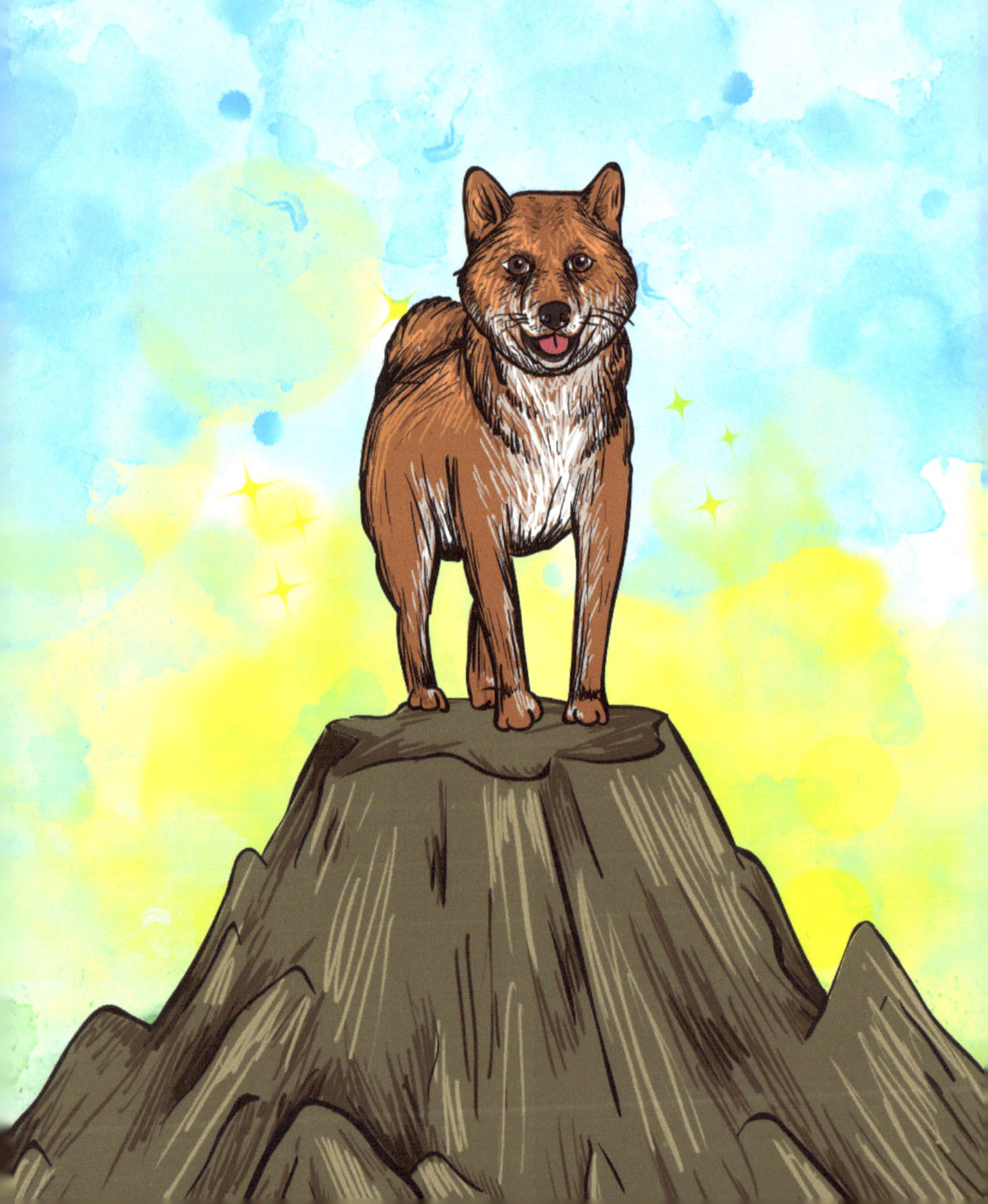

SHIH-TZUS HAVE CURLY, MESSY, KNOTTY FUR.

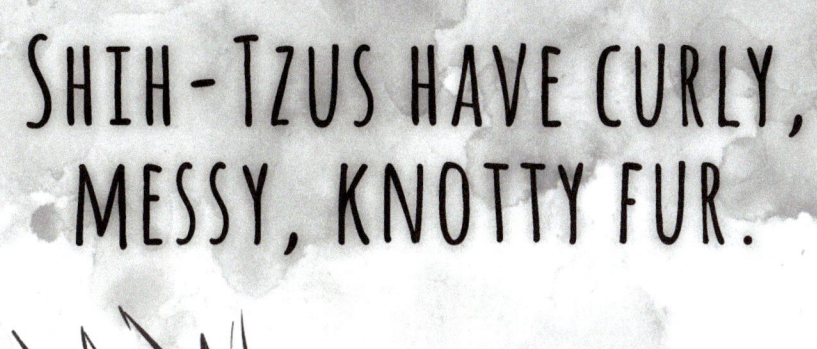

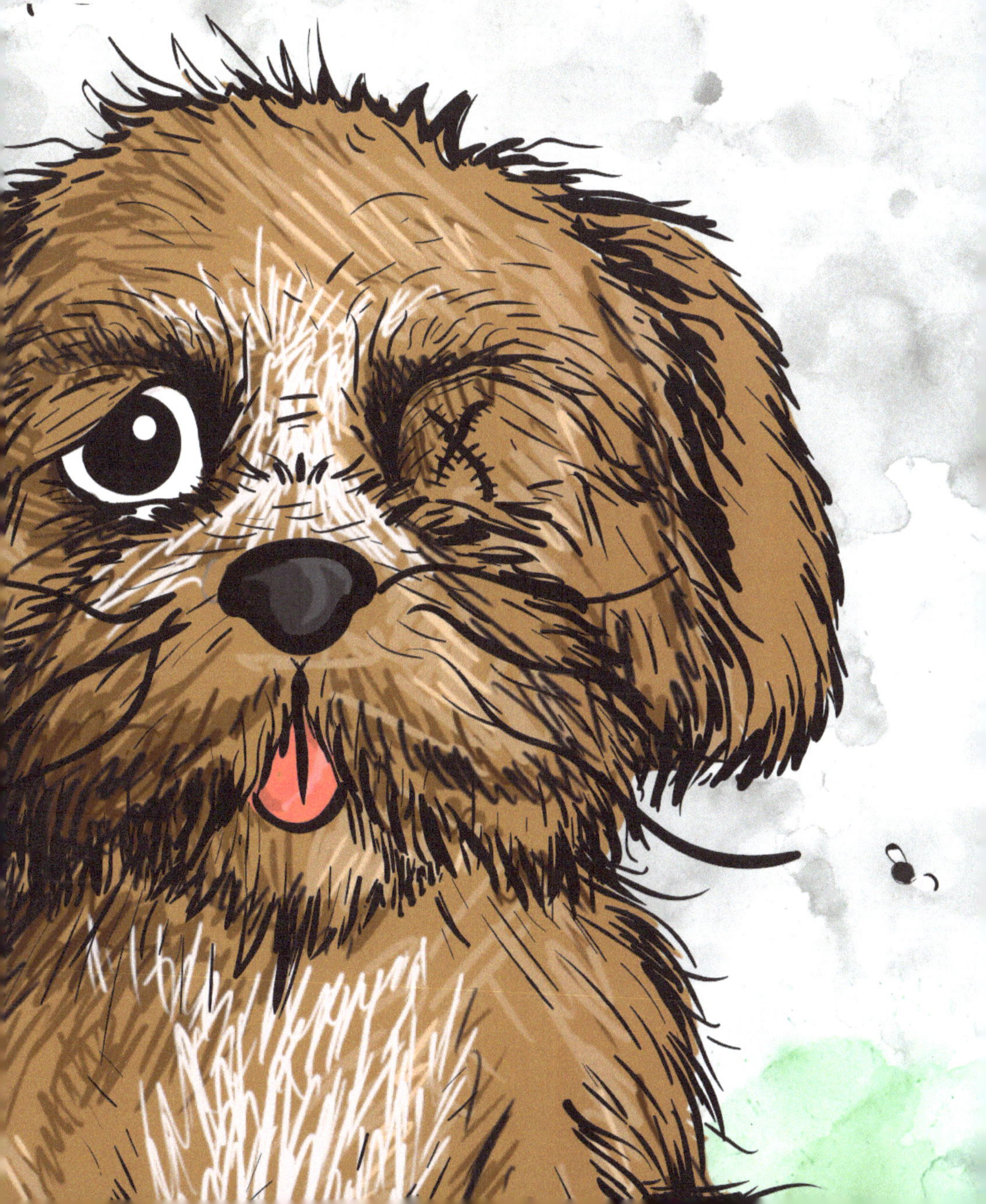

Shiba-Inus have soft and luxurious fur.

Shiba-Inus are quite happy being Shiba-Inus, too.

Sometimes, Shih-Tzus just have to accept that, no matter how hard they try...

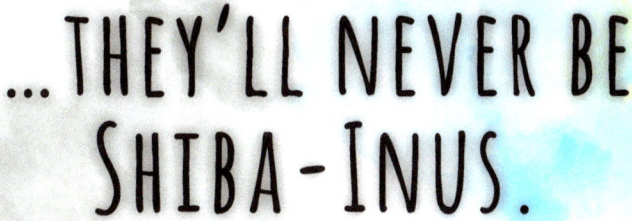

...they'll never be Shiba-Inus.

THEY'LL ALWAYS
JUST BE SMALL

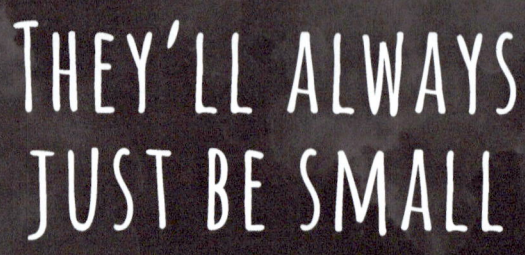

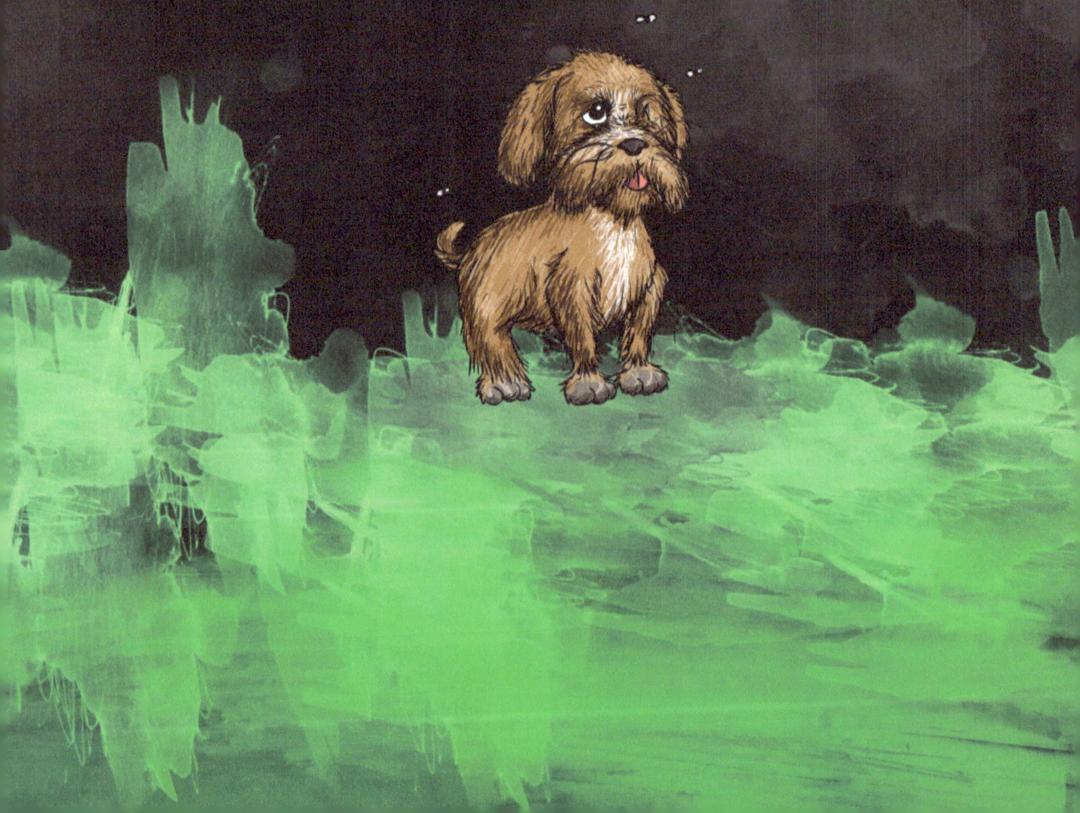

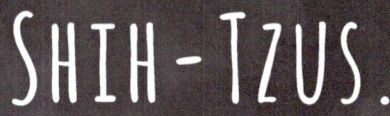

AND SHIBA-INUS TOO.

www.ingramcontent.com/pod-product-compliance
Lightning Source LLC
Chambersburg PA
CBHW042235090526
44589CB00001B/13